W9-APD-370

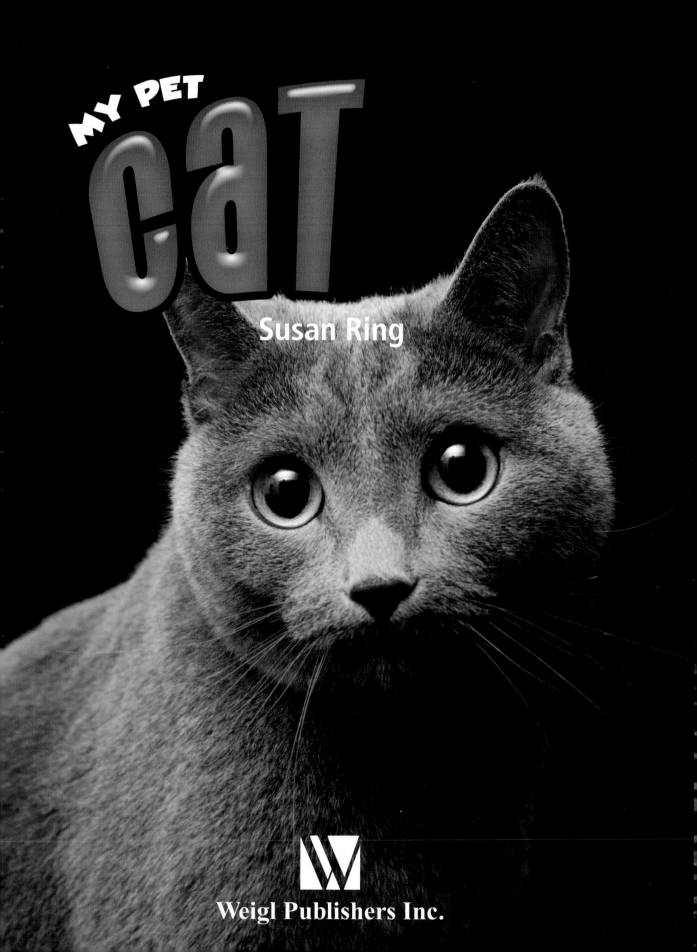

MY PET
CaT

Susan Ring

Weigl Publishers Inc.

Published by Weigl Publishers Inc.
350 5th Avenue, 59th Floor
New York, NY 10118
Website: www.weigl.com

Project Coordinator
Heather C. Hudak

Design and Layout
Terry Paulhus

Library of Congress Cataloging-in-Publication Data

Ring, Susan.
 Cat : my pet / Susan Ring.
       p. cm.
ISBN 978-1-59036-899-2 (soft cover: alk. Paper) –
ISBN 978-1-59036-898-5 (hard cover: alk. paper)
1. Cats—Juvenile literature. I. Title.
SF447.R56 2009
636.8—dc22

2008015819

Printed in the United States of America in North Mankato, Minnesota
2 3 4 5 6 7 8 9 0 13 12 11 10 09

122009
WEP17000

Photograph and Text Credits

Weigl acknowledges Getty Images as its primary image supplier.

Every reasonable effort has been made to trace ownership and to obtain permission to reprint copyright
material. The publishers would be pleased to have any errors or omissions brought to their attention so
that they may be corrected in subsequent printings.

All of the Internet URLs given in the book were valid at the time of publication. However, due to the dynamic
nature of the Internet, some addresses may have changed, or sites may have ceased to exist since
publication. While the author and publisher regret any inconvenience this may cause readers, no responsibility
for any such changes can be accepted by either the author or the publisher.

Contents

Cat Care

Cats are warm, furry, loving animals. For thousands of years, they have been worshiped, loved, and even feared. People are drawn to these cuddly creatures because they are beautiful and mysterious.

Cats are usually very quiet. They do not require much space and do not need to be walked. A cat that jumps, plays, and chases can bring a little piece of the wild into a household.

4

While cats are cuddly, they are also a big responsibility. A cat requires commitment. Properly caring for cats includes giving them the things they need to stay healthy and happy. Cats need fresh water, the right foods, a warm place to sleep, and plenty of exercise. They also need to be **groomed** and taken for regular visits to the **veterinarian**. Another important part of caring for your cat is getting to know her.

Like people, each cat has a unique personality and individual needs. Take time to listen, watch, and understand these needs. When cats are cared for and loved, they return this love in many ways. They can play with us, make us laugh, or comfort us when we are sad.

ZZZZZZ
ZZZZZ

Feline Facts

- Cats purr when they are happy, sick, or in pain. Cats can purr while they inhale and exhale. Some scientists believe that purring is caused by a vibration of vocal cords.
- Cats are the most common pets in the United States, followed by dogs.

- The top three most popular pet cat names in the United States are Tiger, Max, and Tigger. Sam and Kitty are also very common cat names.

yuk!

Pet Profiles

Cats are different sizes, shapes, and colors. Most house cats are mixed-breed cats. This means they are a mixture of different cat **breeds**. Some people prefer **purebred** cats.

There are about 40 cat breeds, many with distinct features. The Turkish Van has waterproof fur. The Manx does not have a tail.

SPHINX

- No hair or whiskers at all
- Wrinkled skin
- The first Sphinx was born in 1966 to two furry parents
- Loves to be watched
- Does not enjoy being the only pet in a household, so it is best to own another cat or even a dog

DOMESTIC

- One of the most common types house cat
- Includes long-haired and short-haired
- Variety of colors, sizes, markings, and shapes
- Variety of temperaments
- General name that includes all **nonpedigreed** cats

PERSIAN

- Most popular breed in the world
- Very long, fluffy coat
- Requires a great deal of daily grooming, combing, and brushing
- Variety of colors
- Flat face and stocky body
- Quiet and loving

SCOTTISH FOLD

- Born with straight ears, but at about three weeks old, ears fold over forward
- Long or short hair
- Variety of colors
- Sweet and loving
- Quickly adapts to change and any environment

SIAMESE

- Very vocal; will meow loudly and often
- Strong, independent, self-assured personality
- Requires much attention
- Sleek, tan body with dark paws, tail, ears, and head
- Large, pointed ears
- Thin, pointed head
- Very intelligent
- Short hair

RAGDOLL

- Large, fluffy body with long, silky coat
- Light-colored fur with darker areas around the face, legs, tail, and ears
- Grooms often
- Requires much combing and brushing
- Very loving
- Laid-back personality
- Gentle with children
- Is a floor cat; not a jumper

From Wild to Mild

Cats have lived on Earth for millions of years. Scientists have found ancient **fossils** of the first ancestor of many of today's big cats, including the lion.

This weasel-like animal, called *Miacis*, is believed to have been the ancestor of present-day **domestic** cats as well.

Domestic cats are related to lions and other "big cats."

The fossils reveal that Miacis lived about 50 million years ago. It took thousands of years for the wildcats of the past to become today's domestic cats.

African wildcats are likely the closest relatives to present-day house cats. African wildcats were domesticated by the ancient Egyptians as early as 2500 BC.

These wildcats would come to people's homes to kill mice for food. The mice ate people's grain, so the Egyptians enjoyed having the cats around. People began to feed and care for the cats that were the most friendly.

eeek!

Ancient Egypt

- Experts believe that cats and humans have shared their homes for about 5,000 years.
- When cats died in ancient Egypt, they were **mummified** and buried with their owners.

- The Egyptian cat goddess, Bastet, had the body of a woman and the head of a cat. She was the goddess of love and fertility.

Life Cycle

It is fun to play with a cute, tiny kitten. It is equally important to spend time with older, adult cats. Throughout their lifetime, cats depend on their owners. From a newborn kitten to a senior cat, your pet's needs will change during her lifetime.

Newborn Kitten

Kittens are born completely helpless. Their eyes are closed and will not open for 8 to 12 days. They cannot walk very well. Instead, kittens crawl. Most of their time is spent sleeping and drinking their mother's milk. Always wash your hands before handling a newborn kitten. Germs on your hands can make a newborn kitten sick.

Four Weeks

At four weeks old, kittens are alert and walking. They are very curious. They explore and discover new things. They still spend much of their day sleeping. They are more independent, but will watch their mother to learn how to groom and use the litter box. Four-week-old kittens love to chase balls, strings, or ribbons.

One Year

Cats are fully grown at one year of age. They are independent and spend more time alone. Still, they will rely on you for their health and happiness. One-year-old cats need help staying fit and energetic. Pet owners should keep plenty of toys around the house.

More than Ten Years

As they get older, cats begin to need more sleep. They are less active. Their hearing and eyesight may begin to fail. Senior cats may still be playful. They may require a special diet, as some foods are hard to digest. Extra nutrients may also be needed.

Living Life

- The average life span of a cat is about 16 years. In 1939 in England, a cat named Puss lived to be 36 years old.
- Female cats usually give birth to four kittens at a time.

Picking Your Pet

There are many factors to consider and research before selecting a pet. These factors will help you choose the best pet to be your furry friend. There are some important questions to think about before picking your pet.

Kittens should not be taken from their mother until they are 12 weeks old.

What Will a Cat Cost?

Many cats in city shelters are just waiting for a good home. These are often cats that have been rescued off the street. Pet stores sell many types of kittens. They cost more than cats from shelters, but will include some basic supplies and the cat will be **vaccinated**. A purebred cat will be the most expensive option. When calculating the cost of buying a cat, be sure to include the costs of toys, food, bedding, and litter.

What Do I Have Time For?

Do you have time to spend with an active, frisky kitten? You may prefer an adult cat, as they require less attention. Long-haired cats must be brushed and groomed at least once a day. Short-haired cats need less grooming. No matter what your cat looks like or how old he is, you will have to feed him, groom him, and clean his litter box every day.

How Will a Cat Affect my Family?

It is very important to find out if anyone in your family has allergies. Bringing a cat into the home may be dangerous for an allergic sister or brother. Think about other pets you already have at home. How will the family dog or hamster be affected by a new cat?

Cat Care

- Every year, Americans spend more than $4 billion on cat food.
- Scientific studies reveal that people who own cats live longer, have fewer heart attacks, and suffer from less stress.
- Many plants are toxic to cats. Preparing for a new cat includes cat-proofing your home. Remove poisonous plants, such as tiger lilies, daffodils, and mistletoe.

Cat Supplies

Before bringing a cat home, you will need a few basic supplies. These include food and water dishes, a litter box, and a comfortable bed. While you may choose to bring your cat home in a cardboard pet box, you can also buy a cat carrier in advance. A large, sturdy carrier can double as a bed.

Put your new cat in one room for a few days. This will help him slowly adjust to his new home.

To protect your furniture, your cat should have a scratching post on which to sharpen her claws. A very young kitten may need a warm hot-water bottle and a ticking clock in his bed. These will help him feel less lonely. Toys are very important to keep your cat active and alert.

Both indoor and outdoor cats need a litter box inside the house. It can be covered or open. The litter box should always be placed away from the cat's bed, and food and water dishes.

Cat beds can be bought at pet supply stores. Many cats are happy sleeping in a cardboard box lined with blankets. The bed should be placed in a warm room, away from drafts. Do not be surprised if your cat ignores the bed you offer her and chooses her own sleeping arrangements. Often, cats need to feel that they have a special spot in the house that is their own.

Cleanliness is important to cats. Once you know your cat's fur type and length, you may buy a brush and comb for grooming.

Toilet Training

- Some cats can be trained to go to the bathroom directly into the toilet. These cats do not use a litter box at all.

Feeding a Feline

Cats are fussy eaters. It is important to vary your cat's foods. Otherwise, she may develop a taste for one food so much that she will refuse to eat anything else.

Never feed your cat dog food. It does not contain enough protein to fulfill your cat's dietary needs.

What Do Cats Eat?

Canned food is available in many flavors and can give your cat all the vitamins she needs. Dry food should also be given. It cleans and strengthens cats' teeth. Most people feed their cats half canned and half dry food for a healthy balance. You may also want to feed your cat fresh food occasionally. Cats love cooked chicken or turkey. If you feed your cat fresh fish, be sure to remove all the bones. Your cat's water dish should always be fresh and full.

How Much Food?

The labels on cat food include feeding instructions. Still, you should be aware of what works best for your cat. If your cat never finishes the food in his bowl, consider giving smaller portions. If your cat gains weight, try feeding him less often. Veterinarians recommend that cats be fed twice a day.

Treats make most cats happy. These foods come in all shapes, sizes, and flavors. Since most treats offer little nutritional value, they should not be given too often.

Fussy Eaters

- Cats need fat in their diet because their bodies cannot produce it on their own.
- Cats need five times more protein than dogs.
- Chocolate is poisonous to cats.
- Most cats prefer their food at room temperature.
- To drink, a cat laps liquid from the underside of his tongue.

Fast and Furry

Whether a simple alley cat or a majestic lion, all cats have certain features in common. Most cats have fur on their bodies to keep them warm.

Cats are fast, **agile**, strong, and smart. Their senses are keen and sensitive. These characteristics help make the cat a great hunter.

A cat's mouth contains sharp, pointed, front teeth that are used for grabbing and ripping meat. Their rough tongue helps them groom and drink.

Even before they can see, kittens use their sharp sense of smell to guide them. A cat's nose can tell him who or what has been in a room before him.

Since cats are **predators**, they need to run fast. Domestic cats can run about 30 miles (48 kilometers) per hour. Cats also have sharp **retractable** claws. The bottoms of their paws are protected by tough pads.

Cats can see in the dark about six times better than humans. A cat's pupils grow very large and round in low light. This allows more light to enter. In bright light, a cat's pupils become narrow slits.

A cat's whiskers are extremely sensitive to touch. Whiskers help cats feel their way through small spaces and dim light. A cat can judge whether his body will fit in a tight space by whether his whiskers fit.

A cat's tail is an extension of its backbone. Cats use their tail for balance and to show their moods.

Cats have very keen hearing. They can move their ears to locate sounds. Each ear can be moved independently and can turn 180 degrees.

Very strong back legs help cats jump onto high surfaces. Cats, along with camels and giraffes, walk by moving both their left legs, then both their right legs. This helps them walk silently and quickly.

Purr-fect Grooming

Cats spend much of their time grooming and cleaning themselves. They lick a paw and, using it like a washcloth, clean their face. Their rough tongues act like combs, pulling out dirt and twigs. Still, sharing the grooming between cat and owner is very important.

Cats do not need baths. Most cats do not like water. Only when cats have fleas will they need to be bathed and shampooed.

Grooming helps a kitten adjust to being handled. It also helps owners check their cat's fur and skin to make sure he is healthy. Regular grooming creates a bond between cat and owner.

Most cats purr when they are being brushed. Regular grooming helps prevent hairballs. When grooming themselves, cats can swallow too much fur. This fur can block their stomachs.

It is important to use the right brush for your cat's fur type. Different fur types and lengths need different kinds of brushes. Once you have found the right brush for your cat, you are ready to begin. Hold the cat on your lap or in front of you on the floor. Slowly look through your cat's fur. Check for **mats**, burrs, and skin sores. Gently brush downward from the head to the tail. After brushing, long-haired cats should be combed with a wide-toothed comb.

Cats' claws must be regularly trimmed. They must be clipped at a certain spot on the claw. This must be done carefully. Ask a veterinarian to show you how to cut your cat's claws before you try it on your own.

feet and fur

- Scratching is a natural instinct for cats. As long as they have claws, they will scratch. Many veterinarians oppose declawing. Cats' claws are part of the toe bone. The operation that removes the claw also removes the last joint of each toe. It is painful because it changes the form of the paw. It also changes the way the cat walks and runs.

- Long-haired cats must be brushed every day to prevent tangles and knots.

Healthy and Happy

Never give aspirin to a cat. Cats can die from eating aspirin or other human medicines.

A healthy cat is a happy cat. Grooming and the right foods will keep your cat healthy. Loving and caring for your cat does a great deal to keep her happy. Regular exercise helps your cat stay fit. Choose a veterinarian that makes you feel at ease. Your veterinarian will answer questions about your cat's behavior and health.

The veterinarian can also give your cat vaccines. These will protect her from common cat illnesses. When your cat is about 6 months old, it should be **neutered** or **spayed**. These operations prevent male cats from fighting and **spraying**, and prevent female cats from having kittens.

Once you know your cat's personality, it will be easier to notice when something is wrong. Take note of pattern changes. Is your cat sleeping more or eating less? Have her bathroom habits changed? Is she drinking more water than usual? A cat is likely sick if she is coughing or sneezing.

Be aware of limping or licking of wounds. These may need veterinary care. Cats are playful and curious. Sometimes, they can get into trouble and hurt themselves. Take some time to make sure your home is safe for your cat.

looking Good

- Cats can develop gum disease and tooth decay. They should have their teeth cleaned by a veterinarian once a year. Special cat toothbrushes and toothpastes also keep your cat's mouth healthy.

- Cats with white and light-colored fur can get a sunburn. It is best for these cats to stay out of the sunlight.

Cat Behavior

Even though cats are very independent, they still enjoy bonding and playing with their owner. Indoor cats need more toys and activities than cats that adventure outdoors. All cats need plenty of love and attention.

A cat's senses are alert, even during naps. Poking or pulling a sleeping cat's tail may result in a scratch.

Cats are smart. They can be trained and disciplined. Sometimes, cats can be naughty. Bad behavior can be gently corrected with a firm "no." A cat should never be hit. A hug or a treat can be given to reward your cat when he has done something good.

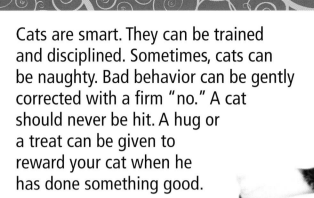

Even though your cat cannot speak, he can communicate with you in other ways. Your cat will let you know when he is happy, upset, or afraid by the movement of his tail. A loud purr usually means he is content. Cats that are grooming usually want to be alone. When a cat rubs his head against you, he is looking for attention.

Pet Peeves

Cats do not like:
- loud noises
- barking dogs
- too much attention
- too little attention
- closed doors
- being moved from a warm lap when sleeping
- having their tails pulled

Cats rub their heads against people or objects. This marks the person or object with the scent glands found between the cat's eye and ear. Your cat will be more comfortable when he recognizes his scent on you. With time, patience, and close attention, you will learn to understand what your cat is saying to you when he meows, purrs, licks, chirps, and hisses.

Cat Quirks

- Some cats go crazy over **catnip**. About 80 percent of cats respond to the herb by drooling, rubbing, purring, and rolling around.
- The sleepiest of all mammals, cats spend 16 hours of each day sleeping.
- When cats are afraid, they often jump to a higher place in the room. Heights allow them to see much more. This makes them feel more secure.

Cat Tales

From presidents to movie stars, many important people have been cat lovers. Famous friends to felines include Daniel Boone, the legendary American frontiersman; Sir Isaac Newton, who discovered the theory of gravity and invented the first cat-flap door; Mark Twain, the author of *The Adventures of Huckleberry Finn*; and U.S. presidents Abraham Lincoln and George Washington.

Of Cats and Men

"The Cat that Walked by Himself" is a fable that explains the personality of the domestic cat. The cat may have become a tame companion, but he still maintains an independent spirit. In this fable, the dog, the horse, and the cow agree to become domesticated. The cat still resists, longing for his wild life. The cat appears at the human's den and says, "I am not a friend, and I am not a servant. I am the cat who walks by himself, and I wish to come into your cave." A deal is made between cats and men. The cat promises to catch mice forever, as long as he is allowed to walk by himself.

From Rudyard Kipling's *Just So Stories*.

President Theodore Roosevelt had a gray cat named Slippers. Slippers had six toes on each foot. Slippers would disappear for days but always returned for large state dinners at the White House. He sat wherever he wished, and visitors at the White House had to walk around him.

From famous cat owners to celebrity cats, these furry creatures have appeared in books, movies, television shows, stories, and fables. Sylvester and Tweety first appeared together in "Tweety Pie," in 1947. This short film earned the Warner Brothers cartoon department its first Academy Award. Sylvester was a kitty with a killer instinct. Audiences watched Sylvester chase his feathered enemy in more than 40 cartoons.

Cat Talk

- About 95 percent of pet cat owners admit that they regularly talk to their cat.
- In 1950, a 4-month-old kitten in Switzerland followed mountain climbers all the way to the top of the 14,691-foot (4,478-m) Matterhorn, in the Swiss Alps.
- During his time as the governor of California, Ronald Reagan signed a bill that made it illegal to kick cats.

Pet Puzzlers

What do you know about cats? If you can answer the following questions correctly, you may be ready to own a cat.

Q Why are cat toys so important?

A A domestic cat still has many of the instincts of the wild. Your pet cat may become restless or depressed if he is bored and inactive. It is important to keep your cat strong, healthy, and energetic with a variety of toys and games.

Q What does a cat use her whiskers for?

A A cat uses her whiskers to determine whether her body will fit in a narrow space.

Q Why must long-haired cats be brushed daily?

A Long-haired cats need to be groomed at least once a day. This prevents tangles, knots, and mats that can be painful and annoying to a cat. Regular brushing also combats hairballs.

Q How often should you feed your cat?

A It is recommended that cats be fed twice a day. The quantity of food may vary depending on your cat's particular appetite. Half of her meal should be canned food, while the rest should be dry food.

Q How do cats communicate with their owners?

A Purring, wagging tails, meowing, and rubbing against their owner's legs are some of the ways that cats tell humans how they are feeling.

Q How long have cats been domesticated?

A Experts believe that cats and humans have lived together for about 5,000 years.

Q When should you have your cat neutered or spayed?

A Veterinarians agree that cats should undergo this operation at six months of age.

Calling Your Cat

Before you buy your pet cat, write down some cat names you like. Some names may work better for a female cat. Others may suit a male cat. Here are just a few suggestions.

Garfield

Fluffy

Smokey

Puss

Ginger

Sylvester

Sheba

Snuggles

Morris

Socks

Frequently Asked Questions

How can I keep my cat cool in the summer?
Cats are good at keeping themselves cool in hot weather. Remember that cats always need to have fresh water available. It may help to keep the blinds closed during the day to block sunlight. A fan blowing in the room can help as well.

Why does my cat scratch the furniture?
Cats need to sharpen their claws. This prevents their claws from growing too long and hurting their paws. While outdoor cats will use trees, indoor cats need a scratching post. Little caps that fit over each claw can also protect your cat, as well as your furniture. Talk to your veterinarian about ways you can work with your cat to help him change this behavior.

Should I give my cat extra vitamins?
Cats that eat good, balanced, nutritious cat food do not need extra nutrients. Some cat owners give vitamins to cats who are pregnant, very old, or under stress. Vitamins should always be given following the advice of a veterinarian.

More Information

Animal Organizations

You can help cats stay healthy and happy by learning more about them. Many organizations are dedicated to teaching people how to care for and protect their pet pals. For more cat information, write to the following organizations.

American Cat Association

8101 Katherine Avenue
Panorama City, CA 91402

Humane Society of the United States

2100 L Street N.W.
Washington, DC 20037

To answer more of your cat questions, go online, and surf the following websites.

Natural History Museum of Los Angeles County

www.nhm.org/cats

Animal Planet Cat Guide

http://animal.discovery.com/guides/cats/cats.html

CatChannel.com

www.catchannel.com

Words to Know

agile: athletic; moves easily

breeds: groups of animals that share specific characteristics

catnip: a plant with sweet-smelling oils

fossils: remains of animals and plants from long ago found in rocks

groomed: cleaned by removing dirt from fur

mats: tangles, knots, and clumps of fur

mummified: preserved a dead body

neutered: made male animals unable to reproduce

nonpedigreed: not having a pure line of ancestors

predators: animals that hunt and kill other animals for food

purebred: animals whose relatives are known and in whom the same traits have been passed on through the generations

retractable: able to withdraw

spayed: made female animals unable to reproduce

spraying: marking territory with urine

vaccinated: injected with medicines that help prevent certain diseases or illnesses

veterinarian: animal doctor

Index